Gluten-Free Desserts

Quick and Easy Delicious Recipes

By

Sophie Miller

Disclaimer

Introduction

Whether you are following the gluten-free diet out of necessity due to a medical condition or you are doing so because of your own choice, it can be a difficult transition. Going gluten-free means that you can no longer eat traditional baked goods like those you would purchase from the bakery at your local grocery store. These goods are typically made with all-purpose flour that is ground from wheat and other gluten-containing grains. Do not worry – just because you have gone gluten-free doesn't mean you have to give up your favorite treats!

There are plenty of gluten-free flour alternatives that make creating your own gluten-free baked goods easy. From simple switches like almond flour and coconut flour to less common ingredients like sorghum flour and tapioca starch, there are plenty of options to choose from. You may not be able to simply substitute a gluten-free flour for traditional all-purpose flour in your existing recipes, but it won't take you too long to get the hang of using these gluten-free alternatives. Before you know it you will be a gluten-free baking master!

For any of you that don't have cups for measurements the following website is a handy resource to find out the weight in grams for each of the recipes, just remember cup sizes are different country to country. www.traditionaloven.com

If you are a newbie gluten-free baker you may not have heard of some of the ingredients used in the recipes. To help you I have compiled a list of some gluten-free ingredients used in gluten-free baking and this book along with a short description. I have also included some information and links as to where you can buy. This is just a small compilation and these items are available in numerous stores and online.

Almond flour

Great in gluten-free baking as it adds essential minerals, fiber and protein. It also gives a lovely taste. This is readily available in stores and online.

US Supermarkets, Amazon, Healthy food stores and iHerb

UK Supermarkets including Lidl and Tesco Amazon, iHerb

Amaranth Flour

Amaranth flour is a protein-rich flour widely used by the Inca and Aztecs. Seeds from the amaranth plant are ground into a fine powder to produce the flour. Although not a grain it produced a grain-like flour gives a nutty and earthy flavor.

US Amazon, iHerb, Healthysupplies

UK - Amazon, iHerb

Buckwheat flour

Buckwheat flour is a high protein and mineral flour that gives a brown tint and nut-like earthy taste to bread. It is not a wheat, despite the name, and is in fact related to the rhubarb plant. Buckwheat is available in most supermarkets and health food stores. It is one of my favorites – I like to grind it up buckwheat and make my own flour. You can purchase the pre-made flour if you prefer.

Coconut Flour

Coconut flour is high in fiber, sweet in taste and soaks up a lot of moisture. It works well with eggs in gluten-free recipes. It is available to purchase in most if not all supermarkets and health food stores. You can also make your own as shown in the recipe for coconut mini loaves.

Flaxseed (Linseed)

This is used to give a recipe the elasticity that is missing with the removal of gluten and is readily available in most supermarkets and health stores.

Flax-eggs

Mix one tablespoon of flax meal (ground up flax seeds) with 2-3 tablespoons of water and leave to 'set' for 10 minutes.

Quinoa Flour (pronounced keen-wa)

Not only is it the oldest cultivated grain in the world, quinoa is also the most nutritious as it is full of iron, calcium and protein. Unlike a lot of gluten-free flours it is does not require a gum, like xanthan or guar, in baking. It is also easy to make your own by rinsing the quinoa in a sieve under cold water. Shake off the excess water and place the quinoa on a baking sheet and bake in an oven for 12-15 minutes at 170C / 350F until dry. Let it cool completely and then grind in a coffee grinder in batches.

Millet flour

Millet flour resembles wheat in texture and appearance. It adds sweetness, nuttiness as well as lightness to baked goods.

US - Bobs Red Mill

UK - Healthysupplies.co.uk

Oat flour

Oats are a hotly debated subject for those with celiac disease or who are gluten intolerant as they are widely cross contaminated with wheat crops. You need to be certain you are buying 100% gluten-free oats, a few farmers have now started milling gluten-free oats. Bobs Red Mill do a line of gluten-free oats which is available to buy online and in store. Some gluten sensitive people are also sensitive to oats so please ensure you can tolerate them before adding to the recipes.

Potato Starch

Potato starch is used for its soft, light rise and to add moisture in baking and can be found on amazon and iHerb aswell as other sites.

Sorghum Flour

Sorghum flour is a slightly sweet and soft flour so is great in baking. It is similar to millet flour.

Tapioca Flour / starch

Tapioca adds texture, structure and gives baked goods a nice chewiness. It is similar to corn flour.

Teff

Teff flour is packed full of nutrients and protein. It is also very high in fiber and is thought to help lower blood sugar levels as well as give energy. It has become quite popular with athletes due to its nutritional values. It can be used in place of wheat flour in recipes.

Xanthan Gum

Xanthan gum is used in gluten-free baking to moisten, thicken, bind and pump up the ingredients. It needs to be used correctly as too much can make bread become heavy and taste artificial.

US -The free from or baking aisles in supermarkets, iHerb, Amazon ,Health stores

UK / IRE / EU - The free from and baking aisles in Supermarkets like Tesco, iHerb and Amazon

Table of Contents

Muffins and Scones

Recipes Included in this Section:

Lemon Blueberry Muffins

Maple Walnut Scones

Chocolate Chip Muffins

Cinnamon Raisin Scones

Lemon Blueberry Muffins

Almond flour is a healthy, versatile ingredient that helps to make this recipe gluten-free.

Prep Time: 15 minutes

Cook Time: 25 minutes

Ingredients:

- 1 1/3 cups almond flour
- 1 cup brown rice flour
- ½ cup tapioca flour
- 1 teaspoon baking powder
- ¾ teaspoon xanthan gum
- ½ teaspoon baking soda
- ½ teaspoon salt
- 1 ¼ cups light brown sugar, packed

- 2 tablespoons canola oil

- 2 eggs

- 2 cups fresh blueberries

- 1 tablespoon fresh lemon zest

Instructions:

1. Preheat the oven to 375°F and line a regular muffin pan with paper liners.

2. In a small bowl, whisk together the eggs.

3. Combine the almond flour, brown rice flour, tapioca flour, baking soda, baking powder, xanthan gum and salt in a mixing bowl.

4. In a separate bowl, beat together the brown sugar, canola oil, remaining warm water, lemon juice and vanilla extract.

5. Whisk in the eggs until smooth.

6. Add the dry ingredients to the wet in small batches and beat until smooth and just combined.

7. Fold in the blueberries and lemon zest.

8. Spoon the batter into the prepared pan, filling each cup evenly.

9. Bake for 22 to 25 minutes until a knife inserted in the center comes out clean.

10. Cool the muffins for 3 minutes in the pan then turn out onto a wire rack to cool completely.

Maple Walnut Scones

These maple walnut scones are simply divine with a hint of sweetness and just the right amount of crunch. Serve them for breakfast, as a snack or for dessert!

Prep Time: 10 minutes

Cook Time: 20 minutes

Ingredients:

- 1 cup sorghum flour
- ½ cup millet flour
- ½ cup potato starch
- 1 tablespoon baking powder
- 1 teaspoon xanthan gum
- ½ teaspoon ground cinnamon
- ½ teaspoon salt
- 1 large egg
- 1/3 cup vegetable shortening
- ½ cup nonfat Greek yogurt
- 2 tablespoons pure maple syrup
- 2 teaspoons vanilla extract
- 2/3 cup chopped walnuts

Instructions:

1. Preheat the oven to 180C / 350F and line a baking sheet with parchment paper.

2. Combine the flours, potato starch, baking powder, xanthan

gum, cinnamon and salt in a mixing bowl.

3. Cut in the shortening using a pastry cutter to create a crumbled mixture.

4. Whisk in the egg, maple syrup, yogurt and vanilla extract until smooth.

5. Fold in the chopped walnuts, stirring gently.

6. Divide the mixture into eight equal portions and drop them onto the baking sheet in rounded mounds.

7. Bake for 15 to 20 minutes until lightly browned on the edges.

8. Let cool for 10 minutes before serving.

Cinnamon Raisin Scones

These cinnamon raisin scones are the perfect breakfast if you are looking for something warm and fluffy but are tired of muffins. Serve these scones hot with fresh butter.

Prep Time: 15 minutes

Cook Time: 20 minutes

Ingredients:

- 1 cup sorghum flour
- ½ cup almond flour
- ½ cup tapioca flour
- 1 tablespoon baking powder
- 3 tablespoons light brown sugar
- 1 teaspoon xanthan gum
- 1 ½ teaspoon ground cinnamon

- ½ teaspoon salt
- 1/3 cup vegetable shortening
- 1 large egg
- ½ cup plain Greek yogurt
- 2 teaspoons vanilla extract
- ¾ cup raisins or sultanas

Instructions:

1. Preheat the oven to 180C / 350F and line a baking sheet with parchment paper.

2. Combine the flours, baking powder, brown sugar, xanthan gum, cinnamon and salt in a mixing bowl.

3. Cut in the shortening using a pastry cutter to create a crumbled mixture.

4. Whisk in the egg, yogurt and vanilla extract until smooth.

5. Fold in the raisins, stirring gently.

6. Put the mixture on to a sorghum floured surface and cut in to round shapes with scone cutter or use a ramekin.

7. Place on baking sheet and cook for 15 to 20 minutes until lightly browned on the edges.

8. Let cool for 10 minutes before serving.

Chocolate Chip Muffins

Coconut flour can be a tricky ingredient to work with because it is highly absorbent but doesn't stick together like traditional flour – just make sure you use plenty of eggs!

Prep Time: 10 minutes

Cook Time: 30 minutes

Ingredients:

- ¾ cup coconut flour
- ½ teaspoon baking soda
- ¼ teaspoon salt
- 6 large eggs

- ½ cup coconut oil, melted
- ½ cup honey
- 1 teaspoon vanilla extract
- 1 cup chocolate chips

Instructions:

1. Preheat the oven to 180C / 350F and line a regular muffin pan with paper liners.

2. Combine the coconut flour, baking soda and salt in a mixing bowl.

3. In a separate bowl, beat together the eggs, coconut oil, honey and vanilla extract.

4. Add the dry ingredients to the wet and stir until well combined. Fold in the chocolate chips.

5. Spoon the batter into the prepared pan, filling the cups evenly.

6. Let the muffins sit for 5 minutes then bake for 25 to 30 minutes until a knife inserted in the center comes out clean.

7. Cool the muffins in the pan for 5 minutes then turn out onto a wire rack to cool completely.

BROWNIES AND BLONDIES

Recipes Included in this Section:

Double Chocolate Chip Brownies

White Chocolate Blondies

Peanut Butter Swirl Brownies

Chocolate Marshmallow Blondies

Double Chocolate Chip Brownies

This recipe for brownies is very versatile – feel free to substitute dark chocolate for the semisweet baking chocolate or add a sprinkle of white chocolate chips.

Prep Time: 10 minutes

Cook Time: 35 minutes

Ingredients:

- 5 ounces semisweet baking chocolate, chopped
- ½ cup vegetable shortening
- 2 large eggs
- 1 cup light brown sugar, packed
- ½ cup plus 2 tablespoons almond flour
- ¼ cup sorghum flour
- 1 tablespoon tapioca flour

- ½ teaspoon salt

- ¼ teaspoon baking soda

- 2 teaspoons vanilla extract

- 1 cup dark chocolate chips

Instructions:

1. Preheat the oven to 180C / 350F and grease a 9x11-inch baking pan.

2. Melt the chocolate and shortening in a double boiler over low heat. Remove from heat and stir smooth.

3. Beat the eggs in a bowl until frothy then beat in the sugar. Blend until smooth.

4. Whisk in the melted chocolate mixture in small batches and beat until the mixture is smooth and well combined.

5. In a mixing bowl, stir together the almond flour, sorghum flour, tapioca flour, salt and baking soda.

6. Blend the dry ingredients into the chocolate mixture until smooth.

7. Beat in the vanilla extract then fold in the marshmallows.

8. Spread the batter in the pan and smooth the top with a spatula or a knife.

9. Bake for 30 to 35 minutes until the brownies are set in the center – do not overcook.

10. Let the brownies to cool completely on a wire rack before cutting.

White Chocolate Blondies

If you aren't a fan of chocolate, these white chocolate brownies may be just the treat you've been looking for!

Prep Time: 10 minutes

Cook Time: 28 minutes

Ingredients:

- ¾ cup white rice flour
- ½ cup potato starch
- ½ cup cornstarch
- ½ teaspoon xanthan gum
- 1 teaspoon baking powder
- ½ teaspoon salt
- ½ cup unsalted butter, softened
- ¾ cup white sugar
- ¾ cup light brown sugar, packed
- 2 large eggs
- 2 teaspoons vanilla extract
- 1 cup white chocolate chips

Instructions:

1. Preheat the oven to 180C / 350F and grease a 9x13-inch baking pan.

2. Combine the rice flour, potato starch, cornstarch, xanthan gum, baking powder and salt in a mixing bowl.

3. In a separate bowl, beat together the butter and sugar until

light and fluffy.

4. Add the eggs and vanilla extract and beat until smooth.

5. Beat in the dry ingredients in small batches until smooth and well combined.

6. Fold in the white chocolate chips then spread the batter in the prepared pan.

7. Bake for 25 to 28 minutes until the blondies are set.

8. Let the blondies cool completely before cutting into bars.

Peanut Butter Swirl Brownies

Peanut butter and chocolate are two flavors that were simply meant to be together – that has never been more evident than in this recipe for peanut butter swirl brownies.

Prep Time: 10 minutes

Cook Time: 25 minutes

Ingredients:

- ½ cup coconut flour
- ½ cup unsweetened cocoa powder
- ½ teaspoon baking soda
- ½ teaspoon salt
- 5 large eggs, lightly beaten
- 1/3 cup coconut oil, melted
- 2/3 cup honey

- 2 tablespoons coconut milk

- 1 teaspoon vanilla extract

- ¼ cup smooth peanut butter

Instructions:

1. Preheat the oven to 180C / 350F and grease a square baking pan with cooking spray.

2. Whisk together the coconut flour, cocoa powder, baking soda and salt in a mixing bowl.

3. In a separate mixing bowl, blend the eggs, coconut oil, honey, coconut milk and vanilla extract.

4. Add the dry ingredients to the wet and blend until smooth and well combined.

5. Spread the batter evenly in the prepared pan and tap it lightly on the counter a few times to release any air bubbles.

6. Microwave the peanut butter for 10 to 15 seconds on high heat until melted.

7. Stir the peanut butter smooth then drizzle over the brownie batter – gently swirl the peanut butter into the batter with a butter knife.

8. Bake the brownies for 25 minutes or so until the center is set – do not over-bake.

9. Let the brownies cool completely before cutting.

Chocolate Marshmallow Blondies

The perfect mixture of sweet chocolate and fluffy marshmallow, these chocolate marshmallow blondies are sure to be a hit.

Prep Time: 10 minutes

Cook Time: 35 minutes

Ingredients:

- ¾ cup white rice flour
- ½ cup potato starch
- ½ cup arrowroot powder
- ½ teaspoon xanthan gum
- 1 tablespoon unsweetened cocoa powder
- 1 teaspoon baking powder
- ½ teaspoon salt
- ½ cup unsalted butter, softened
- ¾ cup white sugar
- ¾ cup light brown sugar, packed
- 2 large eggs
- 2 teaspoons vanilla extract
- 1 cup mini marshmallows
- ½ cup mini chocolate chips

Instructions:

1. Preheat the oven to 180C / 350F and grease a 9x13-inch baking pan.

2. Combine the rice flour, arrowroot powder, cornstarch,

cocoa powder, xanthan gum, baking powder and salt in a mixing bowl.

3. In a separate bowl, beat together the butter and sugar until light and fluffy.

4. Add the eggs and vanilla extract and beat until smooth.

5. Beat in the dry ingredients in small batches until smooth and well combined.

6. Fold in the chocolate chips and marshmallows then spread the batter in the prepared pan.

7. Bake for 25 to 28 minutes until the blondies are set.

8. Let the blondies cool completely before cutting into bars.

CAKES AND CUPCAKES

Recipes Included in this Section:

Chocolate Layer Cake

Lemon Coconut Cupcakes

Simple Yellow Cake

Chocolate Raspberry Cupcakes

Chocolate Layer Cake

This chocolate layer cake is moist and decadent – frost it with your favorite homemade icing or use the quick recipe below. Decorate with fresh berries for a dessert that looks as good as it tastes.

Prep Time: 10 minutes

Cook Time: 35 minutes

Ingredients:

- 3 cups white sugar
- 2 cups sorghum flour
- 1 cup white rice flour
- 1 cup potato starch
- 1 cup cocoa powder
- 1 tablespoon xanthan gum
- 2 teaspoons baking powder
- 1 ¼ teaspoons baking soda
- ¾ teaspoon salt
- 2 cups skim milk
- 4 large eggs, lightly beaten
- ½ cup canola oil
- 1 ½ tablespoons vanilla extract

Instructions:

1. Preheat the oven to 180C / 350F and grease two 9-inch round cake pans.

2. Combine the flours, potato starch, cocoa powder, xanthan

gum, baking powder, baking soda and salt in a mixing bowl.

3. Beat in the milk, eggs, canola oil and vanilla extract until smooth and well combined.

4. On high speed, beat the batter for 2 minutes until light and airy.

5. Divide the batter between the two cake pans and spread evenly.

6. Bake for 35 minutes, rotating halfway through, until a knife inserted in the center comes out clean.

7. Let the layers cool for 5 minutes in the pans then turn out onto wire racks to cool completely.

8. To frost, top one layer with a layer of icing and place the second cake layer on top.

9. Cover the cake with frosting and decorate as desired.

Quick buttercream frosting

- 1/2 cup butter, softened

- 4-1/2 cups confectioners' sugar

- 1-1/2 teaspoons vanilla extract

- 5 to 6 tablespoons 2% milk

Instructions

Whisk the butter until is it creamy and add the sugar and vanilla. Add milk until you have the required consistency. To make a chocolate frosting add ½ cup of cocoa and reduce the sugar by ½ a cup.

Lemon Coconut Cupcakes

These lemon coconut cupcakes are full of flavor from fresh lemon juice and shredded coconut. Frost them with your favorite icing and sprinkle with coconut to serve.

Prep Time: 10 minutes

Cook Time: 20 minutes

Ingredients:

- 1 cup brown rice flour
- 1 cup potato starch
- 1 cup white sugar
- 1 teaspoon baking soda
- 1 teaspoon baking powder
- 1 teaspoon xanthan gum
- ½ teaspoon salt

- 1 cup unsweetened coconut milk

- 1 large egg

- 3 tablespoons coconut oil, melted

- 1 tablespoon fresh lemon juice

- ½ teaspoon lemon extract

- ½ teaspoon coconut extract

Instructions:

- Preheat the oven to 180C / 350F and line a regular muffin pan with paper liners.

- Combine the rice flour, potato starch, sugar, baking soda, baking powder, xanthan gum and salt in a mixing bowl. Stir well.

- In a separate bowl, beat together the coconut milk, egg, coconut oil, lemon juice, coconut extract and lemon extract.

- Add the dry ingredients in small batches and beat until smooth and well combined.

- Spoon the batter into the prepared pan, filling each cup about 2/3 full.

- Bake for 15 to 18 minutes until a knife inserted in the center comes out clean.

- Cool the cupcakes in the pan for 5 minutes then turn out onto a wire rack to cool completely.

Simple Yellow Cake

Whether you are in need of a quick recipe for a birthday cake or you are just craving a deliciously simple dessert, this yellow cake is perfect!

Prep Time: 10 minutes

Cook Time: 35 minutes

Ingredients:

- ¾ cups sorghum flour
- ¾ cups millet flour
- ½ cup tapioca flour
- ½ cup potato starch
- ½ cup arrowroot powder
- 1 tablespoons baking powder
- 2 teaspoons xanthan gum
- ½ teaspoon sea salt
- 1 ¼ cup skim milk
- ¾ cup canola oil
- 4 large eggs plus 1 yolk
- 1 tablespoon vanilla extract

Instructions:

1. Preheat the oven to 180C / 350F and grease two 9-inch round cake pans.

2. Combine the first eight ingredients in a mixing bowl.

3. In a separate bowl, beat together the milk, canola oil, eggs,

egg yolk and vanilla extract.

4. Beat the dry ingredients into the wet in small batches until smooth.

5. On high speed, beat the batter for 2 minutes until light.

6. Divide the batter evenly between the two pans and bake for 30 to 35 minutes until a knife inserted in the center comes out clean.

7. Cool the cake layers in the pans for 5 minutes then turn out onto a wire rack to cool completely.

8. To frost, top one layer with frosting then place the other cake layer on top. Cover the entire cake with frosting.

Chocolate Raspberry Cupcakes

Made with rich chocolate flavor and fresh raspberries, these chocolate raspberry cupcakes are perfect for a special occasion but easy enough to make for any occasion!

Prep Time: 10 minutes

Cook Time: 20 minutes

Ingredients:

- ½ cup sorghum flour
- ½ cup millet flour
- 1/3 cup tapioca flour
- 1/3 cup potato starch
- ¼ cup unsweetened cocoa powder
- 1 teaspoon xanthan gum
- 1 ½ teaspoons baking soda

- ½ teaspoon baking powder

- ¼ teaspoon sea salt

- ½ cup whole milk

- ½ cup warm water

- 2 large eggs, beaten

- 3 tablespoons canola oil

- 1 teaspoon vanilla extract

- 1 cup fresh raspberries

Instructions:

1. Preheat the oven to 180C / 350F and line a muffin pan with paper liners.

2. Combine the flours, potato starch, cocoa powder, xanthan gum, baking soda, baking powder and salt in a mixing bowl.

3. In a separate bowl, whisk together the milk, water, eggs, canola oil and vanilla extract.

4. Beat in the dry ingredients until smooth and well combined – beat on high speed for 2 minutes.

5. Place the raspberries in a bowl and mash gently with a fork. Fold the raspberries into the batter.

6. Spoon the batter into the prepared pan, filling each cup about 2/3 full.

7. Bake for 18 to 20 minutes until a knife inserted in the center comes out clean.

8. Cool the cupcakes for 5 minutes in the pan then turn out onto a wire rack to cool completely. Top with icing and extra raspberries.

COOKIES AND SQUARES

<u>Recipes Included in this Section:</u>

Lemon Squares

Chocolate Chip Cookies

Rice Crispy Treats

Peanut Butter Cookies

Cinnamon Pumpkin Bars

Lemon Squares

Full of fresh lemon flavor, these lemon squares are soft and tender – what more could you ask for in a dessert?

Prep Time: 15 minutes

Cook Time: None

Ingredients:

For the Crust Layer:

- ¾ cup chopped walnuts

- ¼ cup unsweetened shredded coconut

- 5 pitted medjool dates

- 2 ½ teaspoons fresh lemon zest

- ¼ teaspoon salt

For the Top Layer:

- 1/3 cup coconut oil

- 2 tablespoons honey

- 2 tablespoons fresh lemon juice

- 1 teaspoon fresh lemon zest

- 3 drops liquid stevia

Instructions:

1. Combine the walnuts, coconut, dates, salt and lemon zest for the crust layer in a food processor until well combined.

2. Press the mixture into the bottom of a square glass dish that has been lined with parchment paper, spreading evenly.

3. Beat the coconut oil in a mixing bowl until creamy.

4. Add the lemon juice, lemon zest, honey and liquid stevia and blend until smooth.

5. Spread the mixture over top of the crust layer then cover with plastic and chill for 1-2 hours minutes or until set.

6. Remove the parchment paper and cut into squares.

7. Serve cold topped with a shake of icing sugar or coconut.

Chocolate Chip Cookies

Nobody can resist a fresh chocolate chip cookie straight out of the oven and these are no exception! Everyone can enjoy them because they are gluten-free!

Prep Time: 10 minutes

Cook Time: 15 minutes

Ingredients:

- 1 ½ cups brown sugar, packed

- 1 cup sorghum flour

- ¾ cup potato starch

- ½ cup almond flour

- 1 teaspoon xanthan gum

- 1 teaspoon baking soda

- ½ teaspoon salt

- 2/3 cup canola oil

- 2 large eggs

- 3 teaspoons vanilla extract

- ¾ cup semisweet chocolate chips

Instructions:

1. Combine the dry ingredients in a mixing bowl.

2. Beat together the oil, eggs and vanilla extract in a separate bowl then beat into the dry ingredients until smooth and well combined.

3. Fold in the chocolate chips then cover and chill the dough for 45 to 60 minutes.

4. Preheat the oven to 180C / 350F and line a baking sheet with parchment paper.

5. Shape the dough into 1-inch balls and arrange them on the baking sheet.

6. Lightly flatten each cookie and bake for 12 to 14 minutes, turning half way, until golden on the edges but still soft to the touch.

7. Let the cookies cool in the pan for 3 to 5 minutes then transfer to a wire rack to cool completely.

Rice Crispy Treats

These rice crispy treats are simple to throw together and sure to be a hit with the kids. For a little extra flavor, swap out the almond butter for peanut butter!

Prep Time: 15 minutes

Cook Time: None

Ingredients:

- 1 ¼ cups brown rice syrup or ½ cup agave nectar
- ¾ cup natural almond butter
- 2 tablespoons coconut oil
- 1 ½ teaspoons vanilla extract
- 6 cups gluten-free rice cereal

Instructions:

1. Line a rectangular baking pan with parchment paper and set aside.

2. Melt the brown rice syrup in a saucepan over medium heat, stirring, until it begins to bubble slowly.

3. Remove the saucepan from heat and stir in the coconut oil, almond butter and vanilla extract.

4. Stir the mixture gently until it thickens slightly.

5. Pour the cereal into a large mixing bowl and pour the brown rice syrup mixture over it.

6. Gently stir the cereal until it is evenly coated then press it into the prepared pan, spreading it evenly.

7. Cover the pan with plastic and chill until the bars are firm. Cut to serve.

Peanut Butter Cookies

Not only is this recipe gluten-free, but it doesn't require any flour at all! With just a few ingredients you can make a batch of warm, delicious peanut butter cookies.

Prep Time: 5 minutes

Cook Time: 10 minutes

Ingredients:

- ¾ cup white sugar

- 1 teaspoon baking soda

- ½ teaspoon vanilla extract

- Pinch salt

- 1 large egg

- 1 cup smooth natural peanut butter

Instructions:

1. Preheat the oven to 180C / 350F and line a baking sheet

with parchment paper.

2. Beat together the sugar, baking soda, vanilla extract, salt and egg in a mixing bowl until smooth.

3. Add the peanut butter and beat until well combined.

4. Drop the dough in rounded teaspoons onto the prepared baking sheet and lightly flatten with the back of a fork.

5. Bake for 10 minutes, turning half way, or until the cookies are just set.

6. Leave on the tray to set for 10 minutes before transferring to a wire rack to cool.

Cinnamon Pumpkin Bars

These cinnamon pumpkin bars are moist, tender and full of pumpkin flavor.

Prep Time: 10 minutes

Cook Time: 55-70 minutes

Ingredients:

- 1 cup / 100g of Almond Flour

- 1 Banana Mashed

- 1 Cup of Pumpkin Puree

- 1/2 Cup / 125 ml Organic Honey

- 2 Tsp of Cinnamon

- 2 Tbsp Water

- 1 Free Range Egg

- 3/4 tsp Sea Salt

- Spray Oil

Instructions:

1. Pre-heat Oven to 180C / 350F

2. Line a baking dish (a square one preferably) with parchment and spray with oil.

3. Mix the egg, banana, pumpkin, water and honey together in a bowl.

4. Mix the almond flour, sea salt and cinnamon together in a separate bowl.

5. Pour the pumpkin mixture in to the almond mixture and blend well.

6. Pour the combined mixture in to the lined baking dish.

7. Bake for an hour and check, it could take a little longer.

8. My cooking times have varied between 55mins and 1hour and 10 minutes so keep an eye on your oven - It should be golden and a crust should be visible on top.

9. Remove from the oven when done and allow to cool in the dish for 10 minutes before moving to a wire rack. Cut in to 9 pieces, they are nice served warm or cold.

OTHER DESSERTS

Recipes Included in this Section:

Cheesecake

Tiramisu

Easy Apple Crisp

Sticky Toffee Pudding

Cheesecake

Cheesecake is a classic recipe that individuals on the gluten-free diet often have to give up, simply because of the crust. By using gluten-free cookies or graham crackers, however, you can make your own gluten-free crust and enjoy a delicious cheesecake!

Prep Time: 15 minutes

Cook Time: 30 minutes

Ingredients:

For the Crust:

- 2 cup crushed gluten-free graham crackers

- ¼ cup white sugar

- 6 tablespoons unsalted butter, melted

For the Filling:

- 2 ½ (8-ounce) packages cream cheese, softened

- ½ cup honey

- 3 large eggs

- 2 tablespoons milk

- 1 ½ teaspoon vanilla extract

- ¼ teaspoon salt

- For the Coulis

- 250g blueberries (or other berries if you prefer)

- 100ml / 6 tablespoons water

- 2 tablespoons of maple syrup / agave nectar

Instructions:

1. Preheat the oven to 180C / 350F

2. Stir together the crust ingredients until it is well combined.

3. Pour the crust mixture into a 9-inch round springform pan and press it evenly along the butter and about 1 inch up the sides.

4. Bake the crust for 8 minutes then set aside to cool.

5. In a mixing bowl, beat the cream cheese and honey together until smooth.

6. In a separate bowl, beat together the eggs, milk, vanilla extract and salt. Add the mixture to the cream cheese mixture and blend well. Fold in the blackberries taking care not to break them up.

7. Pour the filling into the cooled crust and bake for 30 minutes or until the cheesecake is just set in the center.

8. Let the cheesecake cool then gently remove the sides of the springform pan.

9. Chill the cheesecake for at least 4 hours before serving.

10. Make the coulis by putting the berries in a saucepan with the water and syrup, cook on a medium heat for 2-3 minutes. Take off the heat and allow to cool. You can whizz up to make smooth or leave it as it is.

11. Top the cheesecake with the coulis.

Tiramisu

Tiramisu is the perfect dessert for a dinner party or after a nice dinner with your significant other. By using store-bought gluten-free lady fingers (or other soft cookies), this recipe becomes very easy to assemble.

Prep Time: 15 minutes

Cook Time: None

Ingredients:

- 4 large egg yolks, room temperature
- ¼ cup white sugar
- 1lb mascarpone cheese, room temperature
- 20 gluten-free lady fingers
- 3 ounces strong coffee
- 1 tablespoon dark rum
- Unsweetened cocoa powder

Instructions:

1. Beat the eggs and sugar in a mixing bowl until pale and thick – about three minutes.

2. Whisk in the mascarpone cheese in 4 separate additions, beating well after each.

3. Combine the coffee and rum in a bowl and whisk well.

4. Dip the lady fingers in the mixture then arrange half of them on the bottom of a rectangular dish.

5. Cover the lady fingers with half the mascarpone mixture and arrange the remaining lady fingers on top.

6. Spread the remaining mascarpone mixture over the lady fingers then cover with plastic and chill for at least 1 hour.

7. Dust the tiramisu with cocoa powder just before serving.

Easy Apple Crisp

This apple crisp is easy to throw together and sure to please – if you are looking for a hot and hearty dessert for the whole family, give this recipe a try!

Prep Time: 15 minutes

Cook Time: 45 minutes

Ingredients:

- 6 medium ripe apples
- 1 tablespoon fresh lemon juice
- 2 tablespoons honey
- ½ tablespoon tapioca flour
- 1 cup almond flour
- ¾ cup sorghum flour
- 1 cup light brown sugar, packed
- 2 teaspoons ground cinnamon

- ½ teaspoon ground nutmeg

- ½ teaspoon salt

- ¾ cup coconut oil

Instructions:

1. Preheat the oven to 180C / 350F and grease an 8x11-inch glass baking dish.

2. Peel the apples and remove the cores then slice them thinly.

3. Toss the apples with the lemon juice the stir in the honey and dust with tapioca flour.

4. Stir the apples well then pour them into the baking dish.

5. Combine the almond flour, sorghum flour, brown sugar, cinnamon, nutmeg and salt in a bowl and stir well.

6. Cut in the coconut oil using a pastry cutter to form a crumbled mixture.

7. Sprinkle the mixture over top of the apples then bake for 20 minutes.

8. Cover the dish with foil and bake for another 20 minutes until hot and bubbling.

9. Cool for 15 minutes before serving.

Sticky Toffee Pudding

Though it may look like a cake, this recipe is actually a sticky, decadent pudding. Serve this pudding with a dollop of fresh cream, ice-cream or a scoop of frozen yogurt. This is a gorgeous dessert!

Prep Time: 15 minutes

Cook Time: 20-35 minutes

Ingredients:

For the Pudding:

- 1/3 cup white rice flour
- ¼ cup tapioca flour
- 2 tablespoons teff flour
- 1/3 cup potato starch
- ¼ teaspoon xanthan gum
- 1 teaspoon baking powder
- ½ teaspoon salt
- 8 pitted medjool dates, chopped
- 1 ¼ cups boiling water
- ¼ cup unsalted butter, softened
- ¾ cup brown sugar, packed
- 1 large egg
- 1 teaspoon vanilla extract
- Sea salt as needed

For the Toffee:

- ½ cup unsalted butter, softened

- ½ cup heavy cream

- 1 cup brown sugar, packed

Instructions:

- Preheat the oven to 180C / 350F and grease a 9x13-inch baking dish or six individual pudding dishes / ramekins.

- Whisk together the flours, potato starch, xanthan gum, baking powder and salt in a mixing bowl.

- In a separate bowl stir together the chopped dates, water and baking soda. Let sit for 5 minutes or so.

- Beat together the butter and brown sugar in a mixing bowl until light and fluffy.

- Add the egg and vanilla extract and beat until smooth.

- Beat the butter mixture into the dry ingredients and whisk until well combined.

- Transfer the date mixture to a blender and blend until smooth.

- Add the date mixture to the other ingredients then whisk until smooth and well blended.

- Pour the ingredients into the prepared pan / dishes and bake for 20-25 minutes if using pudding dishes or 30-35 minutes if using a baking dish – the center should be just set. You can insert a skewer or cocktail stick to check also.

- Meanwhile, whisk together the toffee ingredients in a small saucepan.

- Heat the mixture to boiling, stirring constantly and boil over medium-low heat until thickened (about 5 to 8 minutes).

- Drizzle about the toffee sauce over the pudding and serve with ice-cream

Conclusion

After reading this book, you should know that going gluten-free doesn't mean you have to give up your favorite treats. The recipes in this book are proof that gluten-free desserts can be just as tasty (or more so!) than their traditional counterparts. In trying these recipes, hopefully you have found that gluten-free baking is simple and enjoyable – and your family probably didn't mind helping you taste-test the recipes!

I would love to hear your feedback so if you could take two minutes to leave me a review on Amazon I would very much appreciate it. Go to my book page on amazon and click on write a customer review.

I can also be contacted at glutenfreesophie@gmail.com

Thanks for reading and check out my other gluten-free recipe books

1. Gluten-free Vegan

2. Gluten-free Desserts UNDER 200 calories

3. Gluten-free Bread

Printed in Great Britain
by Amazon